NOTES *from* EDITOR

Well! Fall is finally here! Summer is going bye-bye! And its time to bring the cute girl clothes and shoes out! I'm super excited about this issue because we get to spotlight some of the nations brightest, most beautiful, super intelligent women! Yes! I'm all about Girl Power! Women make the world go round!

When God made us He broke the mode! Cheers to all women! This issue is dedicated to my dearest Stephanie and ALL women who have ever fought or lost the battle to domestic violence abuse or breast cancer!

With All The Love My Heart Can Hold,

Jessica L. Mosley, Steward-Owner of The MizCEO Entreprenurial Brand,

Jessica L. Mosley

Jessica L. Mosley

CONTRIBUTORS

CONTRIBUTING
-WRITERS-

SHANICK BARTELL

JACQUELINE MILLER

DELISA WILLIAMS

SANTISHA WALKER, RN

DR. LESLIE HODGE

WHAT'S INSIDE

TABLE OF CONTENTS

Page 6	**Cover Story- Jacqueline Miller**
Page 8	**Introducing MizCEO Brittney McKinnon**
Page 10	**Introducing MizCEO Makini Smith**
Page 12	**Introducing MizCEO Rachel G.**
Page 14	**Introducing MizCEO Tanisha Mack**
Page 16	**Introducing MizCEO Tameka Hope**
Page 17	**Introducing MizCEO Euturvie**
Page 19	**Introducing MizCEO Young Mogul in The Making Lexi**
Page 21	**Introducing MizCEO Jennifer Lucy**
Page 22	**MizCEO Publishing Queen M**
Page 21	**Introducing Joan Wright Good**
Page 27	**Sean D. Young - Cover Story Written By Dr. Leslie Hodge**
Page 29	**Press Release for MizCEO Entreprenuerial Conference**
Page 30	**Marketing Guru Written by DeLisa New Williams**
Page 32	**Your Gifts Will Make Room For You Written by Shanick Moore**
Page 34	**Leora Ellison Written by Jacqueline Miller**
Page 36	**Meet Dr.Bridgette Jenkins by Santisha Walker**
Page 38	**Melanin is A Super Power by Dr.Leslie Hodge**
Page 39	**Meet Kristen**
Page 40	**Dr. Leslie Hodge Inspires**
Page 42	**October Cover Story- Sandra Chaney**
Page 44	**All about Necoya**
Page 46	**Dr. Jerrica Dodd**

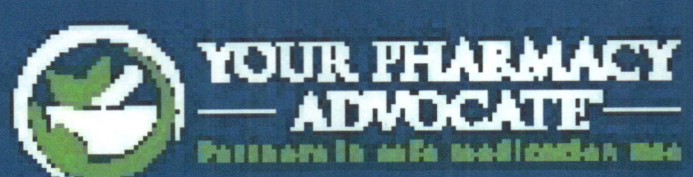

YOUR PHARMACY
ADVOCATE
HAVE A DEDICATED PHARMACIST WORK WITH YOU TO MANAGE YOUR MEDICATIONS, VITAMINS, AND SUPPLEMENTS.
Give us a call today!
1-855-SAFE-MED (1-855-723-3633)
YourPharmacyAdvocate.com

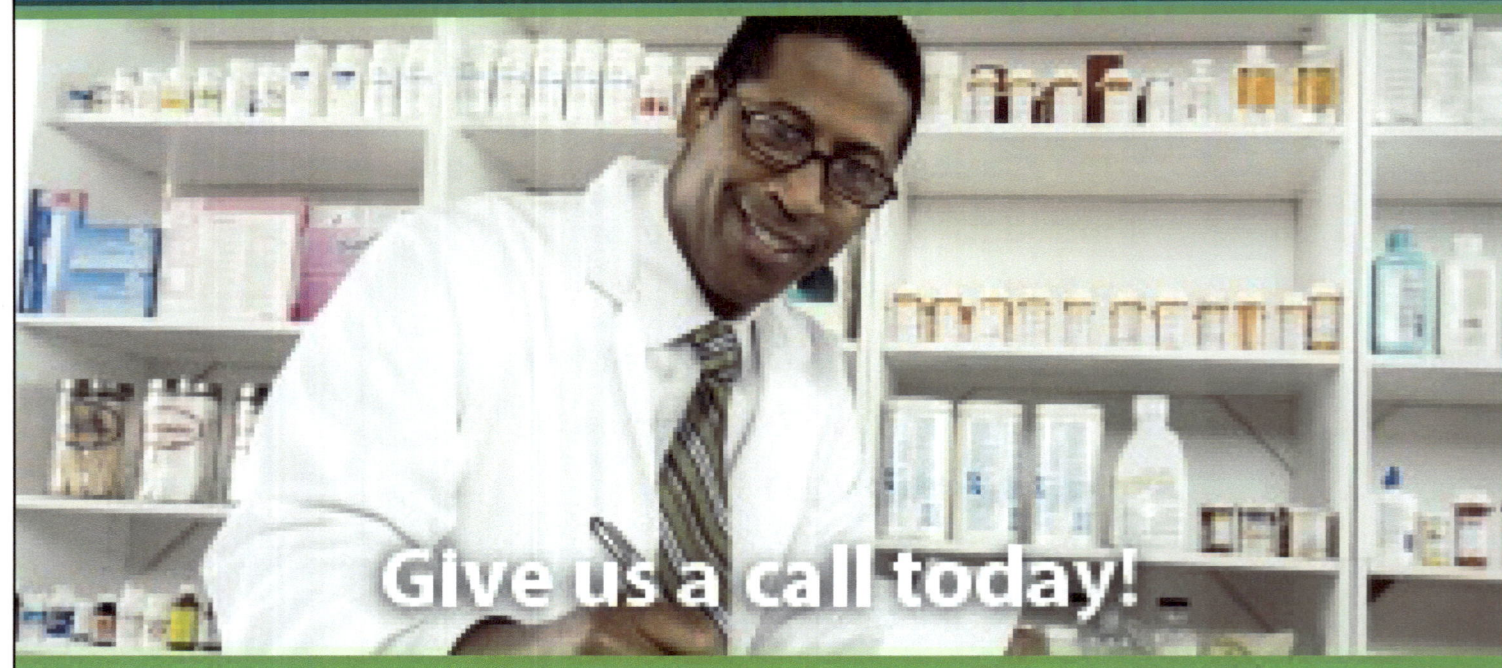

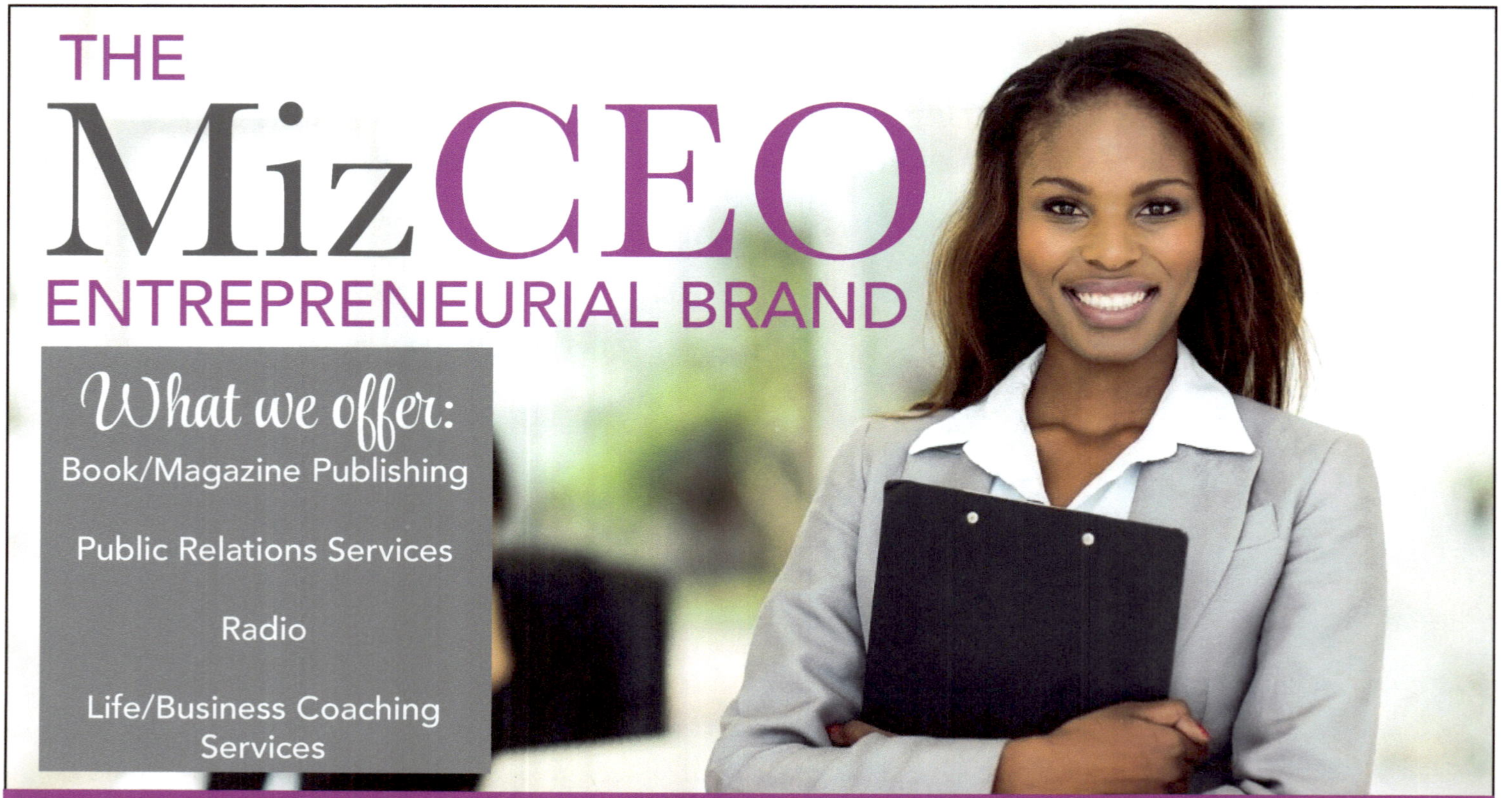

THE
MizCEO
ENTREPRENEURIAL BRAND
What we offer:
Book/Magazine Publishing
Public Relations Services
Radio
Life/Business Coaching Services

FOR THE ENTREPRENEURIAL WOMAN.

Miz CEO
PRESENTS

Queen Status
LIPSTICK LINE

I was challenged by my desire to empower women in their personal lives, while also being an effective resource for them in the business world.

MEET JACQUELINE

By MizCEO Staff

Q: How long have you been in business?
Following a successful 20-year corporate human resources career, I took a leap of faith and started Jacqueline DuJour Enterprises, LLC January 2015.

Q: Why did you pick this particular field to do business in?
Jacqueline DuJour Enterprises, LLC is a service company whose primary mission is to bridge the gap between high-achieving women, their aspirations for life & career excellence and the leading-edge organizations that are committed to fostering exceptional work cultures for women. I picked this field because I believe that women, especially mothers are the backbone of the family structure. Successful work-life integration requires at a minimum, an empowered, confident woman, who can effectively manage a thriving family unit and be a valued asset in the workplace. Combining my diverse human resources, soft skills training, life coaching and facilitator skills, I serve as an expert resource to individual, group, and corporate clientele.

Q: Tell us about a challenge you have had in business and how you have overcome it?
I was challenged by my desire to empower women in their personal lives, while also being an effective resource for them in the business world. This dual role initially seemed impossible to accomplish. I have overcome this challenge by identifying and providing solutions for many of their personal challenges and subsequently identifying and working with organizations that view their workforce as their most valuable asset and are investing in their development, as well as in the workplace accordingly. In addition, my business model allows me to be a resource for aspiring entrepreneurs who are ready to ditch their **faith.**

9-5, and empty nest moms who are seeking to map out the next phase of their lives, by providing them with knowledge, sharing personal experiences and online business resources, before making their own leap of faith.

Q: Why do you feel you have been as successful as you have in your business?

I have never succumbed to a mindset that embraced or found satisfaction in average outcomes and have always understood the importance of a strong work ethic. I have also recognized the importance of collaborations, asking for help when necessary and realizing that a temporary setback is merely a setup for the next, more appropriate opportunity. Most importantly, I continue to understand and accept that my only competition is myself and that self-validation supersedes all others.

Q: Why are you so compelled on seeing other women win BIG?

I am genuine in my belief that when one of wins, we all win. I am and always will be a connector. If I become aware of a resource or opportunity that I can't utilize now but is beneficial to someone else, without hesitation, I think of whom in my space I can pass the opportunity on to. Some have called me crazy, wondering why I am so "helpful." I can only laugh because clearly, they don't know how this thing called reciprocity works. The same energy you put out will affect what comes back to you. There is enough success in this space to go around, so why not be each other's supporter?

Q: So, what's next in 2018 for you? What will be your focus in 2019 for your business?

Expansion of my presence in the corporate and global arena is my primary focus in the immediate future. I am looking forward to using my human resources expertise, coupled with my speaking and life coaching experience to consult with leading-edge organizations and to spread my message to women around the world. Diversity, inclusion, leadership and pay equality for women in the workplace are also areas that I plan to become increasingly more involved in. I aspire to gain more media exposure and to
do more writing for prominent publications as well, which I believe will result in an increase in my speaking engagements.

Fun fact about yourself.

I have performed (sang) on a New York City nightclub stage. I have studied Hebrew, Swahili as well as the violin. Lastly, you can keep the entrees items from the menu; just bring me the dessert cart, especially if it contains quality chocolate!

Q: How can we stay connected with you? (Social media handles)

Facebook: www. facebook.com/jacquelinemogulmomdujourmiller
Instagram: www.instagram.com/mogulmomdujour
LinkedIn: www.linkedin.com/in/thejacquelinemiller
Twitter: www.twitter.com/mogulmomdujour

Final words of encouragement to the female entrepreneur.

Never give up. If this is your dream, go after it as though your life depends on it. Don't define or base your level of success on what you see on social media. All that glitters ain't gold. Be mindful of whom you take advice from. Not all of it may be designed to see you win. In other words, beware of constructive feedback, wrapped in destructive, hidden agendas. Be true to your authentic self. Each day I am reminded of and inspired by these words of wisdom from my Mom: "Do things for others not because of who THEY are, but because of whom I raised YOU to be."

Introducing BRITTNEY MCKINNON

MizCEO: How did you get into your business?
Brittney: I got into my business full-time back in 2014 when I was let go from Government. I started my first business at first as a side hustle / freelancer, just because I needed some extra money, and knew I had a niche I could fill. I had been doing Social Media for government for about 3 years prior, and I used the knowledge, tools and resources that I'd encountered within government to launch B. Carter
Solutions. It was the scariest thing I had done because I was taking this leap of faith with a very small savings, (like $2,000) no direct deposit stability and no healthcare insurance. So, what better thing to dothan continue with my own business? To simplify things, this continued for a while, and the business grew, from one client. One client turned into 3 clients, and 3 clients soon turned into 6 clients. I still wasn't 100% sure if managing other people's social media would be lucrative and sustainable, so, I sat
down and decided how to further my knowledge to grow my business.

MizCEO: How do you handle stress in your business?
Brittney: One thing you learn, is that you will undoubtably underestimate the risks involved with

INTRODUCING MIZCEO BRITTNEY MCKINNON CONT'D

owning a business. You may think that because you don't have to report to the office from 9-5 everyday that you are your own boss. I tell folks all the time to please keep in mind, the "boss" usually has the most stress and most things to worry about, and besides acting as the boss of your company, you still have many other people/factors bossing you around. There are days where stress overtakes my body because I'm doing so much, however, I've learn to delegate things to my team, take a full day of self-care rather it's sitting in pajamas all day watching The Resident, or sleeping in until 11am on a Thursday or my new hobby, going to work out at Orange theory fitness 2-3 times a week.

MizCEO: What is your biggest hurdle you've overcome since becoming a business owner?
Brittney: My biggest hurdle I've overcome since becoming a business owner was to fully rely on God to ºsustain my and my company. I used to struggle with trusting God with my finances in business. Contracts would be lost left and right and it was a very hard struggle for me to keep the faith in Him. There were
times where I lost huge contracts, and would go into panic mode, then couple weeks later, an even bigger contract comes to replace what I had just lost. When you don't have a sustained direct deposit, it's truly scary. You have bills that won't stop, you have a staff to pay and everyday life that requires revenue, but once I've learned to truly put my faith in God with bringing me clients, He has yet to fail me.

MizCEO: What is the biggest achievement you've accomplished with your business?
Brittney: The biggest achievement for B. Carter Solutions was becoming a 6-figure company, generating over 6 figures in revenue which allowed me to hire a full staff of 6, have our very own office space, provide resources to those in need and to fully operate as a Fortune 500 company. My team plays an integral part in the growth of the company, we are now offering a wider range of services on behalf of our clients.

MizCEO:. In your opinion, what is the key to success?
Brittney: Every time I get this question, I always FIRST explains my myths to success. The myth of "being your own boss": You are not your own boss when you own a business. Your customers are your boss. Your bank is your boss. Your fixed costs are your boss. The myth of "independence": Owning a business doesn't make you independent; not needing money makes you independent. As long as you need money, you can't be independent. The key to my success is being able to have the gifts and talents to serve others – that's it. As long as I am happily serving my clients, I know I will always be successful. I love being able to reward myself thanks to the hard work I put in. When you have created a business, you can see the rewards of your hard work, dedication and passion; that makes it worth all of the time and effort you have put into it.

Twitter: @BrittneySCarter
Instagram: @Carterlove
LinkedIn: @BrittneyCarter
Facebook: Brittney Carter McKinnon
Email: bcarter@bcartersolutions.com

INTRODUCING MIZCEO MAKINI SMITH

MizCEO: How did you get into your business?

Makini: I got into my business in 2013 after healing from emotional trauma and mental blockages and wanting to help others do the same. I became a published author after sharing my story in support groups and leaving other women feeling inspired to carry on and do more with their own lives. The program that started my emotional healing was through Sistertalk, founded by Karlyn Percil and featured on Oprah Life Class multiple times. She became my leadership coach and I eventually became one of her mentors in the program helping other women with the same process. I was recommended to watch the documentary "THE SECRET" by a close friend during my healing process in 2010 and a year or so later introduced to Bob Proctor (featured in "THE SECRET"). His wife Linda Proctor and daughter Coleen took me under their wing and encouraged me to get into motivational speaking to inspire women on a greater scale. Linda wrote the foreword for my first book "A Walk In My Stilettos" that shows how I used mindset to heal through my adversities. I continued to break barriers in mindset and glass ceilings in goals and by 2017 became a certified consultant for Bob Proctors company Proctor Gallagher. Today I am a personal development coach, 4 times published author, public speaker andcreator of the A WALK IN MY STILETTOS App (a community for women by womento help you walk in your purpose).

MizCEO: How do you handle stress in your business?

Makini: I handle stress in my business by following systems, being consistent and not taking things personally. Following systems helps you to stay on task. It keeps

me organized. I have to ask myself when I do get stressed out… "Is it helping my situation?" When I start to stress and worry asking myself if that is helpful works.

MizCEO: What is your biggest hurdle you've overcome since becoming a business owner?
Makini: One of the biggest hurdles I have overcome since becoming a business owner is understanding there is no such thing as time management. We don't manage time; we manage what we do with our time. Therefore activity management is more of an accurate statement. We will always have many tasks to do but we have limited time to do it. Making sure the activities I do in a day are goal oriented (aside from time for faith and family) ensures I am not wasting time but investing it into the activities that matter.

MizCEO: What is the biggest achievement you've accomplished with your business?
Makini: One of my biggest achievements thus far in my business has been the global impact of inspiring women to achieve their greatest goals, tap into their full potential and do what others called impossible. I've been able to travel the world and give a voice to women that didn't have one. They are now giving a voice to others. The ripple effect is so fulfilling.

MizCEO: In your opinion, what is the key to success?
Makini: In my opinion, the key to success is having people in your corner that truly supports your success and wants to see you win. That could be a mentor guiding you to save you from lack of knowledge using the wisdom of their success, or a loved one that is there on your down days to motivate you to get back up. You can be in business by yourself but you can't do it alone.

Facebook & Instagram Personal: Makini Smith
Facebook & Instagram Business: awalkinmystillettos
Website: www.awalkinmystillettos.com

INTRODUCING MIZCEO RACHEL G.

Rachel G.

MizCEO: How did you get into your business?
Rachel G: Wow me getting to Coach was by default but God's design. I wrestled with income possibilities as a single mother. So I became a makeup artist on the weekend, and worked in a nursing home during the week. Makeup began to take off for me very well. Then my clients shifted and women with issues started coming to me. They would need advice and what I tell them worked. They kept coming back and started to refer people. People started coming to for advice more so than makeup. so I decided to use my Facebook to try the speaking arena. Who know it would take off. Locally, people started to question my why and God maximized me nationally. I start traveling and now I coach people all over the world.

MizCEO: How do you handle stress in your business?
Rachel G: Of course there is a level a stress that is to be expected with helping people. Taking my time and being around my family helps me, or having my me time daily helps too. Somethings that people think are stressful are not really stressful to me. Maybe because I have lived to learn that it comes with the career path that have chosen.

INTRODUCING MIZCEO RACHEL G. CONT'D

MizCEO: What is your biggest hurdle you've overcome since becoming a business owner?

Rachel G: I had to learn the great flow of business financially. I use my business to provide for my family and brand my business. I had to learn how to manage and structure my live. Most importantly realizing what was important and that everything I face is growing pains. I enjoy taking my mistakes and mastering them with success.

MizCEO: What is the biggest achievement you've accomplished with your business?

Rachel G: Just one??? lol This business I have branded because so many people counted me out and some are them are still counting. Succeeding and actual helping people when others said my theory would not work. Saving marriages, helping broken men and women heal, helping other period! Actually being able to with the help God.

MizCEO: In your opinion, what is the key to success?

Rachel G: Consistency! In due time what you do will come to pass. Just remain consistent and do it, even if you fail. Become the scientist of your brand and recreate it until it works. Your best ideas can come from your mistakes. You'll never know it if you give up and quit!

INTRODUCING MIZCEO TANISHA MACKIN

TANISHA

How did you get into your business?
Becoming an author and publisher was not in my plans. I've always wanted to be a business owner/entrepreneur, but I did not know what I wanted to do. August 2010, I lost my husband in a very public and tragic way. I was told by several different people that I should write a book about it. I wrote my first book and to my surprise it was a success. After that, I continue writing books and I started receiving request from people to help them publish their books. With my experiences, research and continuously learning my field, I started my publishing company.

How do you handle stress in your business?
I am a publisher, so I deal with many different clients on a daily basis, so my job is very stressful. But because of my health and learning self-care, once I start to feel stressed out or overwhelmed, I remove myself from the situation for 5-10 minutes. I have to step back to refocus, pray, and take a few minutes for me. No phone, no computer, no social media, just me and God.

What is your biggest hurdle you've overcome since becoming a business owner?
The biggest hurdle that I had to overcome was minding my business (literally!). We live in the era where we have access to everything and everyone and I became frustrated watching others in the positions where I wanted to be. I was spending money on products, office space and unnecessary things to try and keep up with other businesses. I had to realize that I cannot compare my chapter 1 to someone's chapter 11. I have to continue to stay focus on my business and stop worrying about what others are doing. It takes time and patience to become a successful business. I learned to continue to learn and grow my business, my time will come. You never know what sacrifices another business had to make, all we see is the success.

What is the biggest achievement you've accomplished with your business?
I feel like I achieved several different accomplishments in my business. I am a 3x bestselling author, I have

won several awards for my work, I've published several books for my clients, as well as getting them on the bestsellers list and etc. But one of my best achievements was recently getting my client on the bestsellers list in 3 categories. This was special to my company and myself because this client is in jail and has been for 24 years. My client trusted me fully with his vision, voice and project. It was hard because I did not have access to him every day like I do my other clients. I had to really figure out what was best for him and his book. And now he is a bestselling author and he is very satisfied with the book. Having the ability to help people share their stories through writing is so rewarding.

In your opinion, what is the key to success?
In my opinion, the key to success is determination, discipline, patience and a passion for your business. You cannot want it and don't work for it.

Social Media Handles:
IG: @Authortanishamackinpublishing
IG: @Tanishamackin
Twitter: @TanishaMackin
Facebook: Tanisha D. Mackin

INTRODUCING MIZCEO TAMEKA HOPE

How did you get into your business?
God gave me the vision one day after praying for guidance on a book that I had written and published. I tried ignoring the thought of starting the business but God just would not let me, He only allowed the vision to get strong each day until I finally birthed it.

How do you handle stress in your business?
Whenever I get stressed with my business I pray, go by a body of water and cry out to the Lord. Most of the time after that I start fasting.

What is your biggest hurdle you've overcome since becoming a business owner?
Believing that I can trust and help any & everyone that comes to me for assistance or help.

What is the biggest achievement you've accomplished with your business?
I have reached my goal and desire to help others birth their vision or the fact that I had enough FAITH to step out there and start a business that we didnt even know anything about. We didn't even know how to start the machines.

In your opinion, what is the key to success?
Keeping God first in your life & career, praying without ceasing, staying on one accord with your spouse encouraging each other if your married, pressing through bad & good test together with prayer. Then you strongly need to seek God about everything you do in your career and most of all you have to remain humble and let God do the exalting.

INTRODUCING MIZCEO EUTURVIE EREBOR

Euturvie

How did you get into your business?
I started DOZ Magazine in 2009. I had just come out of a marriage that was abusive, physically, mentally, emotionally and otherwise. I was shattered, and I wanted badly to share my story, as away of easing my pain, but no one was willing to listen without offering some form of criticism andjudgment. So, I took to writing and just pouring out my heart on paper. When I was done, I thoughtit was a good story and that others perhaps would find it both entertaining and inspiring. I had twooptions before me; to submit it to an already established magazine for publication or to create my own magazine and publish my story my way. I chose the latter and DOZ Magazine was born. Butobviously, it takes more than telling one's story to sustain a magazine, and I knew absolutely nothing about managing a magazine, so I shut it down the same year. Then in September 2016, seven years later, DOZ Magazine was relaunched. This time I had more understanding, more clarity of purpose and it has grown and expanded to become, DOZ Network, DOZ Radio, DOZ Show, DOZ Chronicles and DOZ Devotional.

How do you handle stress in your business?
The first time, the way that I handled stress was to shut down the business (hahaha). But now, I know better. Now, I wait on God to tell me what

to do and where to turn, this way when I come face to face with stress I am confident of His support. I face stress confident that whatever is born of God overcomes and my business is born of God and will overcome, so I need not worry. I also handle stress by taking time off work to relax and do leisurely things that I enjoy, that way when I come back to the business I am refreshed, and I can see solutions that I couldn't see before.

What is your biggest hurdle you've overcome since becoming a business owner?

While I can at this moment think of several hurdles that I have overcome since becoming a business owner, I can't say which one is the biggest. But I will share with you one that I considered at the time and still consider to be a major hurdle. When DOZ Magazine re-launched, I obviously began with a new team as the old team had moved on. The new team comprised of a graphics designer with a chip on the shoulder. He was good at what he did, and because of this he was very proud and would make unreasonable demands, and he had a way of doing this at the 11th hour when the work had reached the graphics stage. He knew at this point because we were very close to the release date for the month that I would be willing to concede and give him what he wanted, and this became a huge problem for me especially as I no longer trusted him to deliver the job on time. Whenever it was getting to that time of the month, I would start to become agitated wondering what stunt he would pull this time. Eventually, I had to replace him, and interestingly, once I made up my mind, I discovered that finding a replacement for him was not as hard as I had thought it would be.

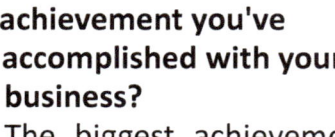

What is the biggest achievement you've accomplished with your business?

The biggest achievement I've accomplished with my business is re-launching DOZ Magazine afterseven years of shutting it down. For seven years, I dreamed of re-launching, but I kept procrastinating and one month became one year and then seven years. So, when eventually I was able to re-launch I didn't take it for granted, I do not take it for granted, and it is till date my biggestaccomplishment as far as my business is concerned.

In your opinion, what is the key to success?

In my opinion, the key to success is discovering your purpose and walking in it. I believe that no one can be truly successful with their ladder leaning against the wrong wall. So, while it's important to climb to the very top of the ladder, it is even more important to be sure that the ladder is leaning against the right wall.

Social Media Handles:
https://www.facebook.com/EturuvieE/
https://twitter.com/EErebor
https://www.linkedin.com/in/eturuvie-erebor-1aa36a86/

INTRODUCING MIZCEO YOUNG MOGUL IN THE MAKING LEXI

Go Lexi!

MizCEO: How did you get into your business?

Lexi: I started Curlanistas as a movement to go with my first book Curly Girls Love Your Curls. I came up with the name and everything. At first my mom hesitated because she said you do know Curlinistas is not a real word, but I really wanted that name and I'm glad I kept it. I wantedto develop my brand to help girls like me with big curly hair. I wanted girls to embrace who they are, to love their hair, to feel empowered, to wear their hair, big, bold and proud. I was teased and I just wanted to help others girls who were going through the same struggles I went through. I taught girls how to love their hair with my books now I want to teach girls how to care for their hair with my line of hair products. I launched my Curlanistas hair line in February 2018, but did a soft launch at the world famous Bronner Brothers Convention in Atlanta in August of 2017, and I sold out the first day. When I let people sample my products they fell in love and I knew I had to keep going to get my brand and get my hair products out there. I wanted to make something that makes caring for your natural hair easier. I would often get in trouble for making hair lotions which I was inspired to make from youtube and instagram. My mom saw that I kept

INTRODUCING MIZCEO YOUNG MOGUL IN THE MAKING LEXI CONT'D

using her coconut oil and she said you really should make your own products. People would also always ask me what I used in my hair. I love playing around with ingredients to see how my hair reacts to them.

MizCEO: How do you handle stress in your business?

Lexi: I handle stress with my business by talking with my mom. She is also my manager and operations manager of Curlanistas; she always has the right things to say and she prays with me. I would say prayer helps a lot. I also take breaks and do something to help get my mind off of whatever is bothering me. I love kickboxing, dancing and listening to music. All these things help. I try not to let much stress me anyway. My mom always says we are too blessed to be stressed.

MizCEO: What is your biggest hurdle you've overcome since becoming a business owner?

Lexi: Learning to manage my time and understanding that I have to make sacrifices to be successful. I cant always go to the movies and hangout when I have goals and events to attend which help promote my business. Also with school making sure my assignments are done on time even when I travel, this was an obstacle for me but now I have a system down and I still make good grades.

MizCEO:. What is the biggest achievement you've accomplished with your business?

Lexi: Knowing that I am inspiring another person to follow their dreams is a major achievement to me. I was part of a huge initiative with Instagram and this book I contributed to Confidence Code for Girls. From that initiative, girls from all over the world were contacting me saying how much I inspire them. Knowing that means the world to me. I've been on TV and in magazines, but knowing I'm helping others feels great. I just want to be an example to others that you can do anything you put your mind to. Its hard work and you may miss parties and other fun stuff but if you want it go get it. I feel so good right now about everything I said I wanted to do is happening.

MizCEO: In your opinion, what is the key to success?

Lexi: The key to success is putting God first, believing in yourself and making goals and then working to make the goals happen. You must believe in yourself and put in the work to make things happen.

INTRODUCING MIZCEO JENNIFER LUCY

MizCEO: Who is Jennifer Lucy at her core?
Jennifer: At the core I am a doer, who is determined to make impact in the lives of people I encounter. I am a servant, visionary, and follower of Christ.

MizCEO: Why are you so passionate about helping other women live their best lives?
Jennifer: I believe every woman is called to be a Changemaker. Whether she's a homemaker, or an entrepreneur that woman has something unique inside of her that God can use to change the world. As women we wear many hats and have many roles. Knowing this, I am determined to help women slow down and reconnect with the source of their strength.

MizCEO: Tell us about your businesses?
Jennifer: My husband Jeff Tyler and I are founders of Tyler Enterprises Inc. Under that umbrella are a few things. I am a professional speaker, author and bible teacher who creates solutions for Changemakers to slow down and study God's word. My latest "solution" is the Changemaker Guide to Studying the Bible. My husband and I are the creators of a journal for couples called "Be Your Own Relationship Goals." Jeff is the founder of a men's apparel line called Good Men do Exist. I am the co-founder of an online boutique.

MizCEO: Where do you see yourself in the next 2 years? 5 years?
Jennifer: Within the next two years I will have had my first Changemaker's Retreat, and have developed more tools and solutions for Changemakers to grow in their relationship with God, and each other through community. I will continue to teach Changemakers how to live missionally through our vision trips where they engage in serving opportunities all over the globe. My app will also be fully developed allowing the Changemaker on the go to connect with God and community online. Within the next 5 years, the Changemaker Retreat along with my Soul Circle pop up study sessions will have happened globally. I will have also trained other Changemakers to lead vision teams to serve, and to lead Soul Circles Bible Study chapters. Prayerfully

JENNIFER LUCY

INTRODUCING MIZCEO JENNIFER LUCY CONT'D

by that time I will be a mom as well. "Soul Circles are meetups where women take over coffee shops and restaurants to learn, discuss and apply basic Bible Study principles while having a great time getting to know one another." I will have also developed studies that women can access via webinar, bookstores and more.

MizCEO: What's next for Jennifer Lucy personally?
Jennifer: Personally I plan to live more authentically one of the messages I teach, and that is the message of "self-care is soul-care." I plan to be more intentional time with God, family, and in solitude. That's how I refuel, and develop creatively. Without this consistent practice I won't be able to effectively do all of what God has called me to do.

MizCEO: What is the greatest lesson that you have learned in business?
Jennifer: The greatest lesson I've learned is the power of consistency and that no today does not mean no tomorrow. Business owners often get discouraged too easily. There is a tribe out there waiting for your gift, or product. While it won't be for everybody, what you carry is for somebody.

Connect with Jennifer via Instagram:
@jenniferlucytyler

MizCEO: How did you get into your business?
WilliamsAndKing: You've heard people boast about their life journey from rags to riches. Well, my mine is quite the opposite, it's more like a riches to rags tale than anything else. I was one of the most successful young black entrepreneurs in my city and my 'empire' included an online bible college, a ministry with my husband and a successful company. I was success personified until the day the bottom fell out and I lost everything including my husband. That was 5 years ago. As an entrepreneur (past or present) you are always thinking of new ways to create wealth. I noticed that in the publishing space there was a lot to be desired as it related to African American books. It bothered me that the work being produced by many publishers was subpar and that there were not many of our stories represented on the shelves of the bookstores. That gave me the idea to start my business.

MizCEO: How do you handle stress in your business?
WilliamsAndKing: It is not easy. I would say there isn't one simple answer to that question. It really depends. Being a mom of three millennials while running a relatively new business is a constant juggling act. Over the past few years, the stress level has been at a constant fever pitch. I contemplated throwing in the towel many times…but God! Thankfully, in those moments, it seemed that He would send an angel to remind me of my purpose. My business partner was one of those angels. She would check in daily and remind me that we were on a divine assignment and that God's vision was much bigger than we could imagine. She would say,

As an entrepreneur (past or present) you are always thinking of new ways to create wealth.

"Stay calm, pray and let God handle the rest, He's the CEO." Besides the calming effect those words would have on me, I walk daily and take Zumba classes. I also participate in a weekly women's prayer time that has centered me and opened my heart to handle whatever comes my way. We can never underestimate the power of prayer and meditation.

MizCEO: What is your biggest hurdle you've overcome since becoming a business owner?
WilliamsAndKing: The biggest hurdle is finances. We have operated this business on a shoe string budget from our own personal funds. We have identified opportunities to grow the business, but we are limited to what we have in our cookie jar.

MizCEO: What is the biggest achievement you've accomplished with your business?
WillamsAndKing: We are a relatively new comer to the space but our reputation has grown. This year we received the Publisher of The Year Award from the Orlando Renaissance Writers Guild in May 2018.

MizCEO: In your opinion, what is the key to success?
WilliamsAndKing: Two minds are better than one. We allow each other to do what we each do best. As the saying goes, iron sharpens iron, we draw on the gifts in each of us and we encourage those gifts to flourish. I have more of the business operations acumen and my business partner is the creative genius. Her posts on creative posts on social media have created a small tribe of followers and we are hoping to build on this until we have a village.

Social media handles:
IG: @thepublishingbabes
Twitter: @williamsandking
Facebook: facebook.com/williamsandkingpublishers. Or @williamsandkingpublishers

INTRODUCING JOAN WRIGHT GOOD

ALL ABOUT JOAN

MizCEO: How did you get into your business?
Joan: As early as I can remember, I have been business minded. As a child, I was a part of the government foster care system and when my mom decided to remove me from the system she sent me to live with my old grandaunt who was an entrepreneur and owner of properties. I would have to accompany her to her cane farm, pimento farm and others where I would assist or watch how business was done. By the age of 14, I liked the independence of having my own money so I would work summer jobs yearly until I dropped out of high school becoming pregnant and homeless at age 17. Hard work and determination had already become my way of life so that one challenge was no match for my destiny. I went back to school and earned a couple of degrees and in 2001 started my first company which was an entertainment & talent management company. Two years later I started a Consulting firm and a clothing boutique and as the years progressed, I rebranded, restarted and reset my businesses, achieving the success I currently have.

MizCEO: How do you handle stress in your business?
Joan: I am a Christian, as such my stress management starts with my faith. The lights are never out in my prayer closet but I also do practical things like exercise and talk to my accountability partners. I have a very high pain and stress threshold so I am rarely bothered.

MizCEO: What is your biggest hurdle you've overcome since becoming a business owner?
Joan: Self-imposed sabotage. I am from the Caribbean, Jamaica to be exact. My husband and last child are Americans, therefore, my household is. My church, my friends, and acquaintances are Americans. 40% of my clientele is Jewish and the other 57% Americans. When socializing and doing business with a mix of cultures you learn a lot. When I just started in business I was afraid to

INTRODUCING JOAN WRIGHT GOOD CONT'D

do the most, say the most or, be the most (impactful) because I feared criticism from my own people. Why did I fear this? I would hear whispers and gossips. During my teething phase, I remember asking a friend for a loan of $20 because she was working and I was not. I was dealing with a family member who was on drugs, raising my children and building a business. She took to texting another friend, a mutual friend of ours to tell the friend behind my back that I was begging. The problem is that she sent me the text she intended to send to our mutual friend instead. Talk about red handed!! Betrayal is a terrible thing. On another occasion, another friend's family member repented for being mean to me because of untruthful, unfounded things she heard by way of my friend, who is her family member. I imposed those thoughts and the not so nice ones that others would say to me growing up like, you will not amount to anything. Fear and betrayal took center stage. It was hard for me to forgive and keep it moving but I did. I had to realize that people are fallible and that tearing down takes fewer muscles than building so it's easy to choose the lesser workout plan. I also reminded myself that those who were talking were dealing with their own demons
and they:

1. Did not have a vision bigger than their critique
2. The vision God gave me, He did not send a memo to them,
3. They were not my source or resource

MizCEO:. What is the biggest achievement you've accomplished with your business?
Joan: My biggest achievement has been the overall growth to a level of President awarded status and major national media attention, such as the Tom Joyner Show. It means a lot coming from a small Island, coming from the humble beginnings that I came from. Kinda like the same feeling I got when I made my first million in sales.

MizCEO: In your opinion, what is the key to success?
Joan: There is NO key to success. What works for 1 person may be disastrous for another, what works in America may be the death of an idea in Hong Kong. Every market is different. I would say the formula for success is: Acknowledging that God is the Source and Resource then making sure you have the: Right Mindset + Right Knowledge (of your product/service/market) + Right product + Hard work + Right platform/vehicle. Then repeat as needed.

Social media handles:
Instagram, Twitter, FB and Snapchat:
@joanwrightgood, FB Public
Page @JoanWrightGoodEmpowers

MEET SEAN D. YOUNG - COVER STORY

THE PHEONIX RISES

By Dr. Leslie Hodge

Want to travel to any place in the world - read a book. Want the underdog to win - write the story. Want proof the phoenix rises — meet the incomparable contemporary romance author,

Sean D. Young. At 12 years old, yes, the tender age of 12, a love for words met the love for writing, when Sean D. Young penned her first literary work — the Easter Play for the youth at her church. No one understood back then the spark lit in the brilliant mind of Sean D. Young. It would be a phone call from her mentor in 2003, asking one question that would change the trajectory of her life - "How is the writing coming?". With only one chapter written, Sean penned the next four chapters of her first book for her mentor to read. Once the final chapters were finished, Sean submitted her completed work for review to BET Books.

Convinced she would receive a rejection letter from BET Books, Sean's plan was to share it with her mentor, and quiet the conversation and expectations concerning her writing. Sean's plan was interrupted with another phone call, and this time the caller was the editor of Arabesque. Arabesque was the leader in publishing of African American-Themed Romance

MEET SEAN D. YOUNG - COVER STORY CONT'D

Novels under BET Books. They called to offer Sean a 2-book contract. Talk about life not going according to plan, Sean released her first book – Total Bliss in 2005.

In 2006, BET Books was sold to Harlequin, another publishing company, where her second book was released. Continuing to write, Sean submitted her third book for review, only to be met with rejection...again.

Believing she was a great writer and hearing from others how great she was, unfortunately was not enough to keep the clouds of doubt from hanging over Sean's head. While managing the changes life brought about, and discovering the "true Sean", coupled with each rejection letter and moving from one publishing house to the next, filled with faith, Sean was determined to push through this chapter of life. She promised the Lord, "I won't quit this time! If you show me what you want me to do, then I won't quit". Just like the phoenix rises, in 2011 Sean released 2 more books – From this Moment and Straight from the Heart ... and you guessed it, with another publishing company - Genesis Publishing.

Sean admits she wanted to quit - but could not. Staying connected and surrounded by those who knew and understood the gift placed inside of her, Sean was encouraged by a fellow author to submit her work to another publisher – Samhain Publishing. Reluctant, yet keeping her promise to God – Sean agreed and submitted her work for review. Samhain Publishing accepted and published 4 more books – The McClendon Holiday Series. Now with a total of 8 published books Sean D. Young had once again risen above what could have kept her down.

The 8th book – A Husband by New Year's was only available for one week, because Samhain Publishing closed its doors. called it quits, walked away from it all, put the pen down for good, is when the phone rang, one more time. This time the caller was Entangled Publishing, asking to reissue not 1, not 2, not 3, but all 4 books in the McClendon Holiday Series. Giving readers the opportunity to experience happily ever after, is why Sean continues to write romance novels, and is a force to be reckoned with. Her ability to evoke an emotional connection from her readers with the characters, is why you will find train passengers on their morning commute with their heads buried in a Sean D. Young book, or the ladies at church clutching their pearls.

Sean is currently working on a new book project with Entangled Publishing. Guaranteed to be another page turner, Sean is committed to keeping her promise and using her gift.

> *"TRUST AND USE THE GIFT GOD GAVE YOU"*
> — SEAN D. YOUNG

Want to know what happily ever after looks like and feels like...read a Sean D. Young book.
Stay Connected with Sean D. Young:
FB: /seandyoung1
IG: @ysdyoung
Twitter: /seandyoung
Website: www.seandyoung.com

Submitted by Dr. Leslie Hodge, founder and operator of Scripts & Beyond, LLC - a medication review and consulting company, is a licensed registered pharmacist and has a passion for people understanding their medications and improving their health. Connect with Dr. Hodge on FB @scriptsandbeyond, IG @dr.hodge or www.drlesliehodge.com.

JESSICA MOSLEY JOIN FORCES IN UNIQUE LITERARY COLLABORATION; EDUCATING, INFORMING & INSPIRING FELLOW WOMEN ON ENTREPRENEURSHIP LIFE

Indianapolis, Indiana (September 15, 2018) – While gender roles have seen a dramatic change over the past half-century, many women are still unaware of the abundant and boundless opportunities that stand in front of them. With a passion for sharing the stories of successful women in the hope that they will inspire others, National Best Selling Author and The MizCEOEntreprenuerial Brand owner - Jessica Mosley is delighted to announce the launch of a ground-breaking and provocative new book titled "The MizCEOEntreprenuerial Book Volume II; 20 Commandments for Women in Business".

The book will be released at the MizCEOEntreprenurial Conference, taking place at Indianapolis, Indiana, on October 12th & October 13th. The Queen of Media - Jessica Mosley has gathered influential female Entrepreneurs from around the world to share the good, the bad, the ugly, and glam of entrepreneurship to women interested in business.

"My book is committed to preparing the world for an inspiring gender equality in the corporate world, by encouraging women to seek out business roles," says Jessica. "There are limitless opportunities for women in business; all they have to do is pursue them and develop the confidence to break all boundaries. Gender imbalance is decreasing but there is still a long way to go; I sincerely hope my book can serve as a strong catalyst for continued change."

To date, the book has garnered rave reviews. For example, one of the Jessica fans commented, "20 Commandments for Women in Business " is the kind of book for women that inspire greatness and shows real-life examples of just how women have attained greatness through strength, determination and a will to succeed. I've always been a person that values investing in your personal and professional growth, and "20 Commandments for Women in Business " is the perfect example of a good investment in your own personal and professional growth as a woman."

Whilst this book will enthrall readers, it will also sustain and empower many women who are on the path to pursuing a career in business. With each book's popularity increasing, interested readers are urged to purchase their copies as soon as possible.

For more information, visit: www.mizceo.com/conference

Media Contact
Company Name: The MizCEO Entreprenuerial Brand
Contact Person: Jessica Mosley
Email: Taylor.jessica46402@gmail.com
Phone: (317)-993-7249
Country: United States
Website: http://www.mizceo.com/conference

MARKETING GURU AND OWNER OF L3 AGENCY

MEET *Larvetta L.* LOFTIN

By: DeLisa New Williams

For this issue of MizCEO magazine, I had the pleasure ofcatching up and interviewing powerhouse womenpreneurLarvetta L. Loftin, Owner and CEO of The L3 Agency - a full service marketing and communications agency focused on influencer marketing and delivering authentic content for brand engagement. For over 16 years, she and her company have been responsible for executing award winning marketing and branding campaigns for **Verizon, Bacardi, Toyota, McDonald's, CVS Pharmacy and The Chicago Community Trust**, to name a few. Trust me when I tell you...she's dope!

DNW: Walk me through your journey of entrepreneurship success with L3?
LL: For nearly two decades, I built an incredible career as a brand marketing strategist, social entrepreneur, media personality, thought leader, and community advocate. I believe you treat others as you want to be treated. My reputation and my character are what makes up my brand success. It is my core values that I care most about---being kind, thoughtful, creative,
authentic, deliberate, and bold. These qualities are what matter for me as a CEO, speaker, community advocate, church leader, mentor, team player, mentee, girlfriend, sister, daughter and the list goes on.

DNW: What do you do to stay on top of your game professionally and thrive in your career for so long?
LL: I believe in staying a student in my business. I also believe in investing in professional and

MARKETING GURU AND OWNER OF L3 AGENCY CONT'D

For this issue of MizCEO magazine, I had the pleasure of catching up and interviewing powerhouse womenpreneur Larvetta L. Loftin, Owner and CEO of The L3 Agency - a full service marketing and communications agency focused on influencer marketing and delivering authentic content for brand engagement. For over 16 years, she and her company have been responsible for executing award winning marketing and branding campaigns for **Verizon, Bacardi, Toyota, McDonald's, CVS Pharmacy and The Chicago Community Trust**, to name a few. Trust me when I tell you...she's dope!

DNW: Walk me through your journey of entrepreneurship success with L3?

LL: For nearly two decades, I built an incredible career as a brand marketing strategist, social entrepreneur, media personality, thought leader, and community advocate. I believe you treat others as you want to be treated. My reputation and my character are what makes up my brand success. It is my core values that I care most about---being kind, thoughtful, creative, authentic, deliberate, and bold. These qualities are what matter for me as a CEO, speaker, community advocate, church leader, mentor, team player, mentee, girlfriend, sister, daughter and the list goes on.

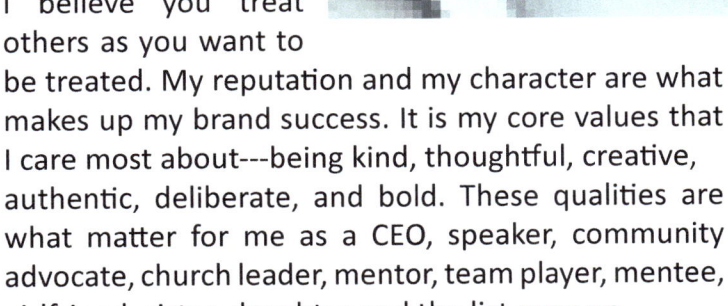

DNW: What do you do to stay on top of your game professionally and thrive in your career for so long?

LL: I believe in staying a student in my business. I also believe in investing in professional and executive development. It allows me to not just work in the business but on the business from the operations side to the client relations side. Most recently, I just completed executive education at Tuck at Dartmouth on Building a Scalable Enterprise and Growing to Scale.

DNW: What sets your business aside from the rest of its kind?

LL: Since 2000, we have operated under a consultancy model that is research-based, relationship-focused, and results-driven. Our history of working in the multicultural and nonprofit segment aligns with our clients' objectives and our agency's philosophy: innovation, collaboration, influence. We listen to our client's needs and develop innovative solutions suited to their unique position. We collaborate with our clients and other agencies and industries to create the best result for our client. We seek out influencers that can deliver our client's message compellingly, thereby making our client more influential. We have the communication acumen and strong relationships with industry influencers and decision makers to surpass our client's' objectives and expectations.

DNW: What advice would you give another aspiring entrepreneur woman?

LL: Take the time to do the research on your business. Allow yourself to fail faster so you gain the knowledge of what not to do. My greatest lessons were my failures. The other thing is be open to pivot your business by selling it or it be acquired by another. What worked 5 years ago, might not work 5 years later, you have to stay on trends and allow the business trends to lead your legacy.

For info on our influencer and communications agency, visit www.theL3agency.com

WHEN YOUR GIFTS MAKE ROOM FOR YOU

By: Shanick Bartell

Beautifully Done
Divaeye Beauty Boutique

Female entrepreneurs are on the rise. Businesses are starting all over the world by women who've made major decisions to step out on faith and use their God given gifts, education, and lessons learned to bring services and products to the masses. When given the task to write about one of these great women, I was led to share the empowering story of a serial entrepreneur named Alice Young. Alice is a jack of all trades as well as a master of them all. She owns a business that literally is a full service one stop shop. Divaeye Beauty Boutique offers the latest fashions and accessories, make-up services, facial and body treatments, natural skincare treatment, and photography. Her story of faith, hard work, commitment, ingenuity, and perseverance is inspiring to say the least.

Me: Your business Divaeye Beauty Boutique offers absolutely everything, how did this all begin?
Alice: It definitely wasn't my initial idea. When I relocated from Trenton, New Jersey to Port Saint Lucie, Florida I was having difficulty finding employment. I had interview after interview with rejection after rejection. I was even told I had to dumb down my resume once.

Me: What changed for you?
Alice: I reached out to my mother, and she told me that that wasn't why I was there. She told me to pray to God for my purpose and my reason for being here. I cried out to God and he spoke to me. I saw a building, called the number, and the very next day, I signed the lease and had my building. I knew what my purpose was and from that point on it was non-stop.

Me: What made you want to start this type of business?
Alice: As a plus size model and someone who loves fashion, I noticed that there weren't any stores in the area that offered fashionable clothing for plus size women. As a licensed beautician, I decided that I would create a space where women can come and get the latest fashion and accessories, glamour make overs, and photo shoots.

Me: Starting a new business can be challenging, what concerns did you have starting?
Alice: My initial concern was that I wouldn't have the support needed in this new place I lived. I was known in my home town of Trenton, New Jersey and here no one knew me. I wanted Divaeye to be a household name. So I decided to get out there and attend every networking event I could. I received so much support from the community. Women would come in, get dressed up, receive make up services and be in tears. They were emotional about how beautiful they looked. I knew even more that I was doing the right thing. My purpose was enhancing beauty. My job was to bring multiple services and products that would enhance the beauty of my clients.

Me: It sounds like a dream come true and seamless process. Were there any obstacles that stood in the way?

WHEN YOUR GIFTS MAKE ROOM FOR YOU CONT'D

Alice: As she bursts out laughing. Oh, Yes! I've had some major obstacles that nearly shut me down. One of the major set-backs I endured was experiencing a flood. My business had to shut down completely during that time. I didn't know what to do at first, but I couldn't stop and give up even if I wanted to. Living in hot Florida and being from the East Coast I thought of offering a cold treat to the community. So I started A Taste of Philly Water Ice business to raise money for the store. We were able to re-open the business and we continue to offer these treats to the community at fairs and events. The other obstacle that was extremely traumatic on me was when I was reported to the State of Florida for practicing make-up with-out a license. I have my Cosmetology license in the state of New Jersey and wasn't aware I was unable to do make up in Florida without an aesthetician license. I could no longer offer these services in my boutique and that rocked my world. It took me to a dark place and thejoy I got from my business I no longer had. It took me a minute, but I couldn't stay down. I picked myself back up and decided to get that aesthetician license. That horrible experience I endured launched me into a field where I can offer so many more services than I did before.

Me: When so many would've thrown in the towel or question if theywere in the right place doing the right thing, what made you keep going?
Alice: I believe it is just who I am. I come from a loving and supportive family with strong women. My mother is a Godly woman who has always been my rock. Whatever she needs she makes it happen even if she has to make it herself. I believe that that is in my DNA and I can't stop or give up. I started my story coming to Port Saint Lucia, FL in a new relationship, I couldn't find a job, started my own business, that business closed temporarily, that relationship ended, one thing after another. I didn't quit and I will not quit. I know there are others just like me and they can make it because I did and I will show them how.

Me: What is next for Alice Young and Dive Eye Beauty Boutique?
Alice: Diva Eye Beauty Boutique will continue enhancing beauty in the lives of our clients. We've also been able to enhance the quality of life of those in the community by supplying job opportunities. We've created homemade all natural beauty products and will continue to host empowerment events, shows, and classes. We won't stop!

Divaeye Beauty will be a household name. This was a small taste into the life of Alice Young. She has shown us that adversaries don't always come to harm us, but may come to help birth that gift inside you. Hardship after hardship didn't break her, but caused her to reinvent herself each and every time. I encourage you to do as Alice did and allow your gifts to make room for you. Alice Young is a licensed aesthetician and owner of Divaeye Beauty Boutique. She offers a full service one stop boutique that offers the latest fashion and accessories, make up services, facial treatments, body treatments, natural skincare, photography, and more. You can find Alice Young on Instagram and Facebook social media outlets at Divaeye Beauty Boutique.

ENTREPRENEUR: LEORA "DENISE" ELLISON

By Jacqueline Miller

COMPANY NAME: SODA POUND CAKES • **LOCATION:** PLANO, TX

How long have you been in this line of business?
19 years as a hobby/residual income and July 2018 as an "official" business.

Why did you select this particular field/industry to do business in?
I was marketing another business and decided to give soda pound cakes as gifts. Then, the light bulb came on after orders for the cakes started to come in. I really enjoy baking soda pound cakes; it's one of my happy places.

How did you decide upon your company's name?
I bake with soda in my pound cakes. Yes, I know, it's an easy answer, but it's factual.

What makes you and your business different from other similar companies?
There may be similar businesses such as cupcakes, cake pops, etc., but I'm unaware of a "soda pound cake" business, and that's what I believe sets me apart. It unique, it's different, and It's my vision from God.

What has been the GREATEST challenge (one that nearly made you want to give up) that you have faced since starting in this business and how you have overcome it?
Self-doubt was my biggest obstacle. Could I really pull this business off and work full-time? Starting a business is challenging and adding doubt to it, the thought of giving up consumed me. I overcame doubt through prayer and perseverance. The Holy Spirit reminded me that "I" cannot do this alone, but with Him all things are possible.

Time management is an area that many people struggle with. How do you find healthy harmony while managing work life integration?
A healthy balance for me begins with devotion and prayer. Also, I create a to-do list every evening for

ENTREPRENEUR: LEORA "DENISE" ELLISON CONT'D

the following day. This helps to track my progress and keeps me accountable. Work life balance is a vital necessity for living a healthy harmonious life while operating a business, and doing something that I enjoy daily certainly helps.

Who are some of the people that have inspired you along this journey and how?
My family inspires me. I know this is a blanket statement, but I'll refrain from giving specific names. However, they and God know who they are. I'm encouraged by people who have a tenacity for life, who have weathered the storms of life – including their marriages, children, and careers. To me, that's inspiring. They have given me unwavering support and encouragement through this journey. They are angels God has encamped around me.

What is a quote or scripture that motivates you and why?
Psalm 27:1 - "A Psalm of David. The LORD is my light and my salvation; whom shall I fear? The LORD is the strength of my life; of whom shall I be afraid?" When I doubt, when I'm fearful... I remember this scripture and receive the peace of God know that he is my light in darkness...my salvation... He is MY strength when I'm weak. Like David, I don't have to fear anything or anyone.

What's next on the horizon for your business in Q4 2018 and 2019?
Q4 2018 - I'm looking to launch wholesale accounts with five (5) corporations. I have a vision to be a vendor at the State Fair of Texas in 2019.

What advice would you offer another woman beginning her entrepreneurial journey?
Write your vision and seek direction from God. Secure your domain name prior to building a brand. You don't want to put in the work to find your desired brand name isn't available. Have a mentor and a support team of 2-3 individuals. There is a difference- mentors tend to be tough but will push you to your end goal. Your support team may be more relaxed. We need both. Don't overshare. Silence is really golden. Remember, it's your vision.

You will be sleep deprived, tired and may want to throw in the towel, so it's imperative that you don't have any joy robbers in your path. Sleep deprivation and tiredness will rob you enough. Know your worth. Don't allow your business to be reduced to a hustle. Be confident in your product. Your customers will pay for it. No is a complete sentence. You must be okay with hearing it.

Take time to enjoy building your brand, laugh a lot and do something that makes you happy daily.

Where can people find more information about you?
- https://www.sodapoundcakes.com
- Facebook: Soda Pound Cakes
- Instagram: @sodapoundcakes

Jacqueline Miller is an international bestselling author, speaker, and certified life coach. She's an expert in empowering high-achieving women to excel in their lives. Her programs provide strategies and resources to obtain clarity, as well as techniques to successfully manage their careers, family obligations, relationships, finances, time management, and self-care. In addition, she is a trainer and consultant for leading-edge corporate clients. Stay connected with Jacqueline Miller by following her on social media. Facebook, Instagram and Twitter @mogulmomdujour as well as on LinkedIn: thejacquelinemiller. Visit her website www.jacquelinedujour.com

MEET DR. BRIDGETTE JENKINS

Is there a doctor in the house?

Dr. Bridgette, you are a very accomplished woman who has been recognized for your service within the nursing profession, as an educator, humanitarian and leader; as well as serving as a mentor and coach for younger nurses and a mother of three adult children, grandmother of two grandsons. How do you balance it all?
While I am so grateful for my life, my amazing children and grandchildren, and my career, it has truly been a constant balancing act. Maintaining a well-balanced life is essential for your happiness, health, productivity, and overall well-being. There have been times that I have been "off balance" as a result of this imbalance my health has been compromised. This has caused me to be more intentional about maintaining a sense of balance in every area of my life.

Being a woman in leadership and operating your own organization, how do you prioritize your health & total wellness?
Because I operate in so many different roles and because I have been diagnosed with multiple autoimmune diseases, prioritizing is crucial for me to maintain my overall health & wellness. So the first thing that I do is, rest my body. There was a time that I accepted every invitation. I literally sit and decide what is important and what is not and I adjust my calendar accordingly. I purposely block an entire weekend and day during the week off for rest and relaxation.

What does self-care look like for Dr. Bridgette?
Oh, I have a routine. The most important part of my self-care routine is prayer and meditation. I use this time to express to God my joy and gratitude for the day, for life, for my health, for my business and my job, and for my family and my friends. Another important element of my selfcare routine is getting enough rest & sleep. I recently stopped working in bed. This was important for me because everything was always in my reach. And I was always tempted to reach over and grab the iPad or the laptop and do some work or answer an email when I should have been asleep. Because I suffer with insomnia, I have made it a point to rest even if I don't go to sleep. This means the lights are off, the room is cool, the TV is off, nothing is in my bed, the sheets are pulled tight and I'm diffusing lavender or

MEET DR. BRIDGETTE JENKINS CONT'D

frankincense to help me relax. Another selfcare activity that I think a lot of business women and leaders forget to do is to enjoy life. Spend time with family and friends doing things that do not involve work. My grandson and I go to the movie at least once a month, I hang out with my friends 2-3 times a month, and I set some time aside for some me time (time that I spend alone doing what I like to do like shopping, getting a massage or reading a book).

As a healthcare professional, what advice would you give women seeking ways to naturally heal and overcome health challenges?
I wrote about this topic in my book, Bounce Back: Tips for Overcoming Adversity, Life Challenges, & Setbacks. I wrote "achieving optimal health is a prerequisite to a high- quality lifestyle. Being in optimal health does not mean there is absence of disease, or alleviating symptoms associated with a particular disease process. It simply means that there is balance physically, emotionally, spiritually, socially and intellectually. If you have a certain diagnosis, is it controlling your life or keeping you from working, going to school, enjoying family and friends or doing what you love? If you answered yes, then you are out of balance. You should examine what caused this imbalance. We all have risk associated with acquiring a disease. There are modifiable risk factors. These are the things that we can change, like diet, smoking, sedentary
lifestyle, and being overweight. Then there are non-modifiable risk factors. These are things that we cannot change such as age, gender, race, ethnic group, family history and genetic composition. What is important to remember is to control those things that can be controlled and manage the things you can't. Here are a few things that can help you achieve optimal health: see your healthcare provider at least once a year, make better food selections, drink more water, maintain an active lifestyle, maintain a healthy weight, practice stress management, get adequate sleep, and listen to your body."

Do you believe there is a connection between your health and successfully operating in the entrepreneurial realm?
Absolutely! Your health is a vital component of running a successful business. If you get sick, who is going to manage the business while you are in the hospital? More than likely your business will suffer. As entrepreneurs our days are filled with appointments, meetings, and events that we don't even have time to eat a decent lunch. We have resorted to eating a burger and fries while driving to our next appointment. This is not good. An entrepreneur needs to be healthy in their mind and body to operate a successful thriving business. You also need to be healthy to enjoy the fruits of your labor, hard work and success.

How can our readers connect with you?
Facebook: Dr Bridgette
Instagram: dr_bridgette
www.drbridgette.com

So tell us a fun fact about Dr. B.
Although I'm very reserved, I'm the life of the party. I love to dance, have fun and see other happy and having a good time.

MELANIN IS SUPER POWER!

By Dr. Leslie Hodge

Melanin is an illumination of God's brilliant creation

- Lasha Tennyson

Throughout history, skin color has been used to trick and create division among families, communities and perpetuate self-hate. In 1712 Willie Lynch wrote a letter to slave owners entitled The Making of the Slaves, which suggested that planting discord between light skinned and dark-skinned slaves, would have a lasting impact for at least 300 years. In 2012, Lasha's eyes were opened to the realities of colorism that still plagued our country and world, after attending the taping of The Oprah Winfrey Show's How Colorism Affects People Around the World.

What happens when history sings a song that you refuse to sing? What happens when you recognize the narrative about skin color and self-love must change? You create a collective voice, force, movement to express self-acceptance and pride for all people of color. You create IdeniTees.

Lasha Tennyson, founder and operator of IdeniTees, is a southern woman from Camilla Georgia, who grew up hearing her grandmother recite the infamous quote, "You are not better than anyone, but you are just as good". It would be those words along with her faith in Jesus Christ that propelled the Florida A & M University (FAMU) alum to embrace herself completely.

IdeniTees was created to inspire people of color to embrace their superpower, melanin. Melanin Rich, She's Born With It, Best Makeup Ever, Botox? Nah Just Melanin are a few of the messages found in the first collection from IdeniTees, fittingly named Melanin.

Lasha Tennyson is committed to providing an avenue to inspire others to embrace the beauty found in every hue and every shade. IdeniTees is changing the song and narrative about skin color for the present generation and the generations to come.

Contact Information
Website: www.ouridenitees.com
IG: @idenitees_
FB: @idenitees
FB Link: www.facebook.com/IdeniTees/

Dr. Leslie Hodge, founder and operator of Scripts & Beyond, LLC - a medication review and consulting company, is a licensed registered pharmacist and has a passion for people understanding their medications and improving theirhealth. Connect with Dr. Hodge on FB @scriptsandbeyond, IG @dr.hodge or www.drlesliehodge.com.

MEET KRISTEN

MEET KRISTEN

MizCEO: Why did you get into business?
Kristen: Business called me. I needed to find a way to do what I was passionate about for a living. My calling is to empower, encourage and connect with women. So, I started my own talk show and production company. This was I could produce and own content that reflected my mission and calling.

MizCEO: How do you handle stress when it arises in business?
Kristen: When stress arises, I know that I have taken too much of the control. It means that I need to re- surrender my business back to God. He gave me the ideas, the vision and He gives me the provision to fulfill the mission. When stress rises up, I take a moment to breathe, get clear and remember who is truly in control.

MizCEO: Tell us about one of the biggest hurdle you have had in business.
Kristen: My biggest hurdle that I've overcome is self sabotage. I've told myself no when God wants to say yes. I've talked myself out of blessings. I've mishandled relationships due to pride, ego and insecurities. Today, I believe that goodness that God has for me and inside of me. I believe God wants to use me to bless others and He wants to use others to bless me.

MizCEO: Tell us about one of your biggest achievements in your entreprenuerial journey.
Kristen: My biggest achievement is completing a second season of my show, The Positive Controversy with Kristen Pope.

MizCEO: One key to success in business.
Kristen: The key to business is having a clear vision, a dope, committed team, prayer, full surrender and belief in yourself.

Dr. Leslie Inspires

Tell us why you decided to go in to business for yourself?
I've always had a passion for people and wanting to help them understand their medications, while improving their health. I selfishly loved seeing the expressions and reactions of people as they learned new information and hearing about the improvements in their health. Working in the retail setting of pharmacy for over a decade, enabled me to see firsthand the gaps that existed between patients and their medications. Instead of just observing the need, I decided to create a solution - Scripts & Beyond, LLC, where the motto is A Pharmacist Focused On YOU™. Scripts & Beyond is a medication review and consulting company which specializes in providing one-on-one medication therapy management services. The personalized services are provided by pharmacists, who use their clinical expertise to review the current medication regimen, recommend medication alternatives and lifestyle changes and help create a plan for each patient to reach optimal health outcomes. I wanted to provide a service where each patient knew decisions were being made with them, and not for them. I wanted them to experience being focused on, considered, and heard, thus creating a peace of mind that the prescription and over-the-counter medications being used are safe, appropriate and costeffective.

What does it take to be a successful business owner?
Prayer. Preparation. Prioritizing. But, it all begins with prayer! Praying for Godly connections, opportunities, and resources. Preparation to effectively and efficiently serve the client and establish collaborations and partnerships. Properly prioritizing what has to be completed by the owner, compared to what can be done by someone else or at another time. It is also important to connect with people who do well or with ease, the tasks that are more difficult. Focus on developing personal strengths, and making them even stronger.

You're an author now. Why did you decide to be a contributing author?
Becoming an author has been a goal of mine for some time. I reached that goal in May 2018, when my first book At The End Of The Day: Take It Personally was released. Interestingly enough, I accepted the offer to

DR. LESLIE HODGE CON'TD

become a contributing author before I even started my own book. When the opportunity presented itself, I was immediately drawn to the idea of collaborating with other business women, fellow believers, and creating something that would allow us to collectively share our thoughts and ideas. The idea of creating a resource for entrepreneurial women with other entrepreneurial women was an opportunity that I knew was packaged as a blessing.

What are you currently working on?
I am preparing for the launch of Reflections Coaching & Consulting, LLC this fall. I will merge my 14 years of corporate leadership and training, with my expertise in healthcare, to empower high achieving men and women to properly manage the stresses from their high demanding careers, explore their internal aspirations, while creating a work, life, health and wellness balance. Services will be provided 1-on-1, group, face-to-face or virtual. Special programs and services are created for corporations and small businesses. Scripts & Beyond, LLC is continuing to make strides in becoming top of mind for medication management services for individuals and families who need assistance with ensuring their medications are safe, appropriate, and affordable. Also, the Hey Girl! Wellness Check is continuing to rollout. It is a call to action health and wellness initiative, created to help women of all ages take an active role in knowing their health status. The first component of the Hey Girl! Wellness Check focuses on physical health. Women are encouraged to know their health status in 7 areas : blood pressure, blood glucose, mammogram, pelvic exam/pap smear, cholesterol, immunizations and eye, ear, and teeth. Encouraging and equipping women to take an active role in their health, can be the difference between life and death. Helping women have the conversation with each
other and checking in with each other creates accountability and responsibility. Not sure how to start theconversation, just start by saying Hey Girl!
Lastly, I am also working on my 3rd book, where I am one of the co-authors, providing a pharmacist's perspective on our role in healthcare. The book is slated for release in early 2019.

What is a mantra that you live by?
I actually live by two: 1) It always seems impossible until its done and 2) Every expert was once a beginner

Are you a big supporter of the next woman?

If so, why?
Yes indeed! I know it's a cliché, but I love seeing women excel and do great things. I love seeing women overcome obstacles and setbacks. I love praying for women and watching God move on their behalf. I love seeing women reclaim that which they thought was lost. I love seeing women grow from level to level. I love cheering women on! Call me, I keep the confetti ready so we can celebrate!

What female celebrity inspires you?
I am inspired by none other than our former First Lady, Michelle Obama. I had the pleasure of hearing her speak earlier this year, and the words of wisdom that spewed from her mouth into an arena filled with men and women from all walks of life, planted seeds that will yield fruit to feed not only this generation, but generations to come. She truly left an impact on my life that will last a lifetime. I'm fascinated by her ability to not only say go high, when others go low, but to literally go high when others go low. I love how her belief in God her support of her husband and family never waivered, even in the face of adversity.

What should we expect from you in 2019?
I'm truly excited about 2019! I really feel like the sky is the limit. I am a big vision board person... I believe in writing the vision and making it plain. I believe in that life and death are in the power of the tongue. With that being said, I am speaking that 2019 will be even greater than 2018...and 2018 has been amazing. 2019 is going to be the year of intentional impact. I am speaking that you should expect to see me on nationally syndicated television shows. I am speaking that you should you expect to hear me on nationally syndicated radio shows. I am speaking that you should expect to see me on a national book tour. I am speaking that you should expect to see me and hear me speak from different platforms and panels across the world. I amspeaking that you should expect great things from Dr. Leslie Hodge!

How can people stay connected?
They can stay connected by visiting
www.drlesliehodge.com or
www.scriptsandbeyond.com
FaceBook @drlesliehodge,
@radioshowwithdrhodge, @scriptsandbeyond
Instagram @dr.hodge, @dr.hodge_newbook,
@radioshowwithdrhodge or @scriptsandbeyond

SANDRA CHANEY - COVER STORY

COMPELLING CHANGE AGENT

NON-PROFIT | GRANT STRATEGIST

SPEAKER, COACH, BESTSELLING AUTHOR

DOMESTIC VIOLENCE AND SEXUAL ASSAULT EXPERT

Sandra Chaney directs her coaching and non-profit advisories from distinct platforms largely derived from her multi-faceted exposure spanning the full gamut and range of businesses and organizations – from IBM to Fannie Mae to her signature consultancy while founding and running her own non-profit.

From those exposed to it, her approach is deemed invaluable – where relevancy and viability produce measurable impacts. Her grants writing proficiency, grounded in her role as an in-demand federal level grants reviewer for nearly two decades (since 2000), has also conferred her coveted referral status as a 'take care of business' resource. Clients attest that Sandra Chaney provides "THE Works" with 360o of effective insight into evolving non-profit constructs. Accordingly, she has secured some $15 million (+ plus) in grant awards for public, private and philanthropic organizations over the last 15 years. When Coaching and Training (individual (1-on-1), Team, organizational or for partnerships/consortiums) Sandra matches capacity to discern content with capacity to effectively convey its relevancy – thus, compelling change agent.

Beyond her live coaching and workshops, Sandra's versatility now expands to access through virtual coaching via her customized webinars and podcasts. Her focused intent, and now proven forte', is to reorient and redirect vested organizations, initiatives and programs in sustainable ways that often evolve ahead of increasingly unprecedented market

Select Awards Recognizing Sandra Chaney's Leadership 2018

2018
Brave, Bold and Beautiful –
Women Leaders Who are Not Built to Break Also featured in their Spring 2018 issue of Unbreakable Women Leaders Magazine – a personal growth and lifestyle guide.

2006
Maryland Top 100 Women nominee
recognizing high -achieving Maryland women making an impact through their leadership, community service and mentorship.

2004
Fruit of Her Hand Award (Atlanta, GA)
tribute to women who have risen above their circumstances to make real differences in their communities.

factors. Such foresight balances the dynamics of a 360o overview with in-depth considerations that establish Sandra Chaney as a definitive asset and resource offering effective:
Coaching| Grant Writing | Grant Reviews | Workshops | Webinars Leadership Training | Program Development | Business Redirect/Engineering

Her non-profit trade primer, The Inside Secrets for Getting Money for Your Non-Profit, which was release both in print and electronically summer 2018 and reach bestseller status on amazon in four categories, will reset standards for 'how-to' funding guides. Concurrent with this release, Sandra will add to her service array as a Certified Author Coach.

ALL ABOUT NECOYA

Necoya. Necoya. Necoya.

Beautiful, smart, and intelligent. She's definitely on her way to BIGGER and so much more! She's publishing books, gracing magazine covers, winning awards, and taking over the scene! We had the opportunity to sit and speak with this phenomenal woman to see what's going on in this last quarter in 2018 in her business.

MizCEO: Tell us why you decided to go in to business for yourself?
Necoya: My entire career has been working in associations planning conferences, tradeshows & special events. In 2008, I worked for an association that was going through a lot of changes including lay-offs. At that point, I'd been doing a lot of research and reading up on starting an event planning business and fear of a layoff prompted me to do it. So in 2009 All About You Event Management was born!

MizCEO: What does it take to be a successful business owner?
Necoya: One must have several characteristics to be a successful business owner. You should be: hard working, dedicated, have perseverance, open-minded, flexible, patient, open to (constructive) criticism, goal-oriented, driven and resilient.

MizCEO: You're an author now. Why did you decide to be a contributing author?
Necoya: I decided to be a contributing author so that I could share my story and help someone who may be on the fence about stepping out on faith with starting their business. I love being a mentor and sharing my experiences with others so that they can learn from them.

ALL ABOUT NECOYA

MizCEO: What are you currently working on?
Necoya: Right now I'm wrapping up my 2018 Mornings are for Mimosas Wedding Workshop Series. This workshop was designed for brides & grooms to help get them started in the wedding planning process so that they can be equipped with the right questions and expectations when going into meetings with their vendors.

MizCEO: Tell us about a time that you wanted to give up but didn't.
Necoya: The past year has been a challenging one for me. While running my business, I was also working a full-time job (like many of us do). Well I was traveling a lot for my job which had me away from home and missing activities and milestones with my son. Then on top of all of that, two of my team members (from my business) quit in the same week; while we were in the middle of planning an event. I was completely OVER IT. But I knew that I couldn't give up. So, I took a couple of days to speak to my mentors, write down my thoughts and goals and pray. I realized that I was doing a lot of things wrong as far as grooming and cultivating my team members. So I started over from scratch and now I have a new team which will officially start at the end of this month. They will have a seat at the table and will have input in all areas of the business so that they know they are a part of the big picture.

MizCEO: What is a mantra that you live by?
Necoya: "I am at peace with all that has happened, is happening, and will happen." I am a firm believer that EVERYTHING happens for a reason and contributes to our growth.

MizCEO: Are you a big supporter of the next woman? If so, why?
Necoya: My goodness, yes! I hate the stereotype that says women, especially black women, don't support each other. If I can push and encourage another woman to be greater, a better person, to follow her dreams and to be a winner, in my eyes that makes us all winners.

MizCEO: What female celebrity inspires you?
Necoya: I know this is cliché, but Oprah Winfrey is a huge inspiration to me. She is a great business owner, supporter of others in her industry and she has a true "rags to riches" story that everyone can relate to in some way, shape or form.

MizCEO: What should we expect from you in 2019?
Necoya: My wedding workshop, Mornings are for Mimosas will make its debut in Miami in January. I'm also working on a tips & tricks for planning your wedding e-book.

MizCEO: How can people stay connected?
Necoya: You can find me on Instagram/Twitter/Facebook/Pinterest under
@aayouevents or #aayouevents

DR. JERRICA DODD
Faith Walker

Dr. Jerrica Dodd is a pharmacist, entrepreneur, speaker, and leader. She is a woman of grace, class, strength, and determination. She is a woman on fire! She knows what she wants and isn't taking no for an answer. To know her is to love her. She's one who doesn't wait for things to happen; she makesthings happen! This is exactly why she went in to business for herself.

Dr. Dodd has paid the cost to be the boss! She has always been an over-achiever! She's always been the one that went the extra mile. She holds a Doctor of Pharmacy degree from Florida Agricultural and Mechanical University, a Master of Science in Pharmacy Administration from The Ohio State University, and a Master of Science with a focus in Applied Pharmacoeconomics from the University of Florida. She completed an ASHP accredited residency at the Wexner Medical Center at The Ohio State University.

Dr. Dodd is a woman that walks by faith and not by sight! After having an exceptional career that has expanded over two decades as a pharmacist, Dr.Dodd took a great LEAP and transitioned into full time entrepreneurship. She has held roles in Medical Affairs and Regulatory Affairs. Prior to her time in the pharma industry, she managed a hospital pharmacy, and has had experience in retail pharmacy. Truly experience is the best teacher. And because of her background, she is more than equipped to run a full service pharmaceutical business.

Dr.Dodd is a believer in being a forever learner. In so much that she recently completed and received a Nutrition Health Coaching Certificate from the Institute of Integrative Nutrition. Currently, she is enrolled in the Institute of Functional Medicine and her goal is to introduce a functional medicine perspective to the pharmaceutical management of member patients of Your Pharmacy Advocate, LLC.

Dr. Dodd is an ordained and licensed minister and served for 6 years at the Global Leadership Christian Center in various roles on the ministry leadership team. Jerrica is the managing member of JD3 Enterprises, LLC and Jerrica Speaks, LLC. and her most recent start-up is Your Pharmacy Advocate LLC. YPA exists to close the gap on medication risks allowing prescribers and patients to manage health better. YPA allows pharmacists to be partners in safe medication use, and Dr. Dodd often says, "everyone needs a pharmacist in their life at some time or another."

DR. JERRICA DODD

Dr. Dodd enjoys living her life to the fullest! She believes that ONLY what you do for Christ will last! She is a stern believer in serving her fellow man. She does that in various ways of philanthropy.

Please connect with Dr. Jerrica Dodd through the following social media outlets:
Facebook: Your Pharmacy Advocate
Linked In: Your Pharmacy Advocate
Instagram: yourpharmacyadvocate
Twitter: pharma_advocate

MizCEO

FOR THE ENTREPRENEURIAL WOMAN　　　　　　　　　　　OCTOBER 2018

GET YOUR BOOBIES CHECKED!

The MizCEO Entrepreneurial Conference 2018

MEET THE PHENOMENAL
Sean D. Young